THE PORTAGE POETRY SERIES

Series Titles

Silent Letter
Gail Hanlon

Bowed As If Laden With Snow
Megan Wildhood

Always a Body
Molly Fuller

New Wilderness
Jenifer DeBellis

Fulgurite
Catherine Kyle

The Body Is Burden and Delight
Sharon White

Bone Country
Linda Nemec Foster

Not Just the Fire
R.B. Simon

Monarch
Heather Bourbeau

The Walk to Cefalù
Lynne Viti

The Found Object Imagines a Life: New and Selected Poems
Mary Catherine Harper

Naming the Ghost
Emily Hockaday

Mourning
Dokubo Melford Goodhead

Messengers of the Gods: New and Selected Poems
Kathryn Gahl

After the 8-Ball
Colleen Alles

Careful Cartography
Devon Bohm

Broken On the Wheel
Barbara Costas-Biggs

Sparks and Disperses
Cathleen Cohen

Holding My Selves Together: New and Selected Poems
Margaret Rozga

Lost and Found Departments
Heather Dubrow

Marginal Notes
Alfonso Brezmes

The Almost-Children
Cassondra Windwalker

Meditations of a Beast
Kristine Ong Muslim

Praise for
Silent Letter

"Brisk, honed, graven as talismans, but somehow fluent and sensual, always carried by a most subtle sprezzatura—Gail Hanlon's poems offer so much of what I want from poetry: one person's brave whistling in the dark, a song that mystery can't help but envy and give an answer to. I sit here this morning with them, feeling more than alive. I'm sure they will make you feel the same."

—David Rivard
author of *Some of You Will Know*

"Gail Hanlon's poems usher us into worlds within worlds: the intimate space that holds two lovers; travels with a sister to visit an ailing mother; and the reverberations of loss alongside a continual sense of discovery. Hanlon's calligraphic style and sureness of touch allow her to startle us and dazzle us by turns. Her poems radiate energy and vibrant life; to read them is to partake of a bracing beauty."

—Jennifer Barber
author of *The Sliding Boat Our Bodies Made*

"How sad I felt when I got to the end of *Silent Letter*, realizing there were no more of these poems! Gail Hanlon's masterful, uneasy mixture of ghostly epistles, imagistic memoir, and involute but plainspoken metaphysics sketch a quiet wilderness of self, a grief-land of beautiful questing and questioning. Each poem, dagger thin and rarely longer than a page, measures itself, skeptically but heroically, against the seeming perfection of silence and speechlessness, wondering, 'What is the world / without language?' before committing to the task at hand: 'You track the answer, / willing to be wrong.' But the poems are never wrong, just full of wonderful questions, 'How to read— / left to right or right to left? // Sunwise or moonwise?' and a longing 'to make absence visible,' which she almost does."

—Gregory Lawless
author of *Dreamburgh, Pennsylvania*

silent
letter

GAIL HANLON

Cornerstone Press
Stevens Point, Wisconsin

Cornerstone Press, Stevens Point, Wisconsin 54481
Copyright © 2023 Gail Hanlon
www.uwsp.edu/cornerstone

Printed in the United States of America by
Point Print and Design Studio, Stevens Point, Wisconsin

Library of Congress Control Number: 2023933973
ISBN: 978-1-960329-00-4

Cornerstone Press titles are produced in courses and internships offered by the
Department of English at the University of Wisconsin–Stevens Point.

DIRECTOR & PUBLISHER   EXECUTIVE EDITOR
Dr. Ross K. Tangedal   Jeff Snowbarger

SENIOR EDITORS
Lexie Neeley, Monica Swinick, Kala Buttke

PRESS STAFF
Ellie Atkinson, Patrick Fogarty, Angela Green, Jordan Hansen, Cal Henkens, Brett
Hill, Julia Kaufman, Amanda Leibham, Cat Scheinost, Maria Scherer, Taylor Schmidt,
Cash Van Stiphout, Matt Vancik, Abbi Wasielewski

For my sisters, brothers, and friends

Also by Gail Hanlon:

Mirabilia

SIFT

Contents

— One —

— Two —

— Three —

Be within be within in.

—Gertrude Stein

— One —

In Theory

I like lipstick in theory
and the names

of lipsticks, especially
Cherries in the Snow.

I say her name over
and over, the way we wrote

our names as girls
sealing ourselves in serifs.

One of these days I expect
to find you doing coke

in a sparkly shirt
she says. This doesn't

seem like the sort of life
you'd be leading.

She's a little
out of season.

I pray the rosary of her spine
irreverently

the shadows of snowflakes
flickering like dark birds

over the torn up pages
of the white sheets

wanting to break
into beauty like a ripe

pomegranate multiplies
in jewels.

A traveler in the Tarot—
the Magician or the Fool—

one arm raised to draw down the stars
or stepping over a cliff

all my belongings tied up
in a handkerchief on a stick.

Golden Record

In love I'm that record they sent out
into space in 1977 in the Voyager
to tempt extraterrestrials.
Sprouting music and the sound of whales
and jungle chatter with a red and yellow halo
ripping around my flaming body
notes springing from every meridian
a tiny heart tattooed at my third eye
and a search light spinning over my crown.

A Step Nearer to Them

That I knew I was wasting
my life, that it gave me more

lightness. More hooky. That I found
a book or two on women

with wings in the *LRB*.
That all was already lost—

a kind of papaya-flowered pleasure
papering the view. From there

a step back and a step
toward. Longing to proceed.

That conjunctions could generate
in medias res put me in the thick of it

hardly a moment's emptiness.
A tabula of little importance.

That I'm still fizzling, shaken,
sugared, and bright even as I am

failing the I-am-not-a-robot
test on a regular basis.

Reticent

Twombly's edges
like radical line breaks

where the caterpillar feels
the air blindly

neurons flicker-fusing
to make absence visible.

Sound visible.

Blindly. Wavers. Stutters.
Into charged territory—a threshold.

The extra margin in a Japanese
garden. Sand beyond sand.

Compelled, I pay attention
drawn to anyone who

stutters, who   feels so much
the way she did when we

were in love—her hesitation so
reverent, eyes dark chapels.
*

Reluctant to speak,
from the Latin reticere.

What kind of writer is that?

Trying to eat my way into
the future with a gold-covered

chocolate Ganesha,
clearer of obstacles, what else

to do? That ritual and the usual combing
over words, wondering why they're so

obscure, even to me, why
it's so hard to recognize clarity.

From Observation

Today's word is *mooncalf*:
daydreamer, absent-minded

person, fool, or simpleton.

Not knowing what words to use
for Simon's paintings, I'm

stunned into silence like she so often
was, her pupils shining ink.

In North Sea High Tide
shaky skeletal lines

like a rough ladder of waves or
a trellis of thought.

Surf nested in the troughs
suggesting and erasing stories.

What would plein air writing be?
I'm ham-fisted, all my words

backing up. Nothing lost on me.

What's My Line?

Everything's a potential concert, the judicious, erratic timing of the birds, the meta-crash of a metal ladder on a gutter. A long minute passing. A match in the dark deploying disparate objects, eliminating visible brushstrokes, a kind of petition, yet another kind of dream, an event of relation. Thoughts floating past as provocative essays. A woman opening a window to feel the humid salt air on her face. Inside the flower's hold, the bee hears nothing, meshing with the drone of the surf. Staggers out, as Bashō says.

End Now or Cancel

She's well enough
then not well at all.

It has happened
before. Will it

happen again?
Or is this the last

time? If this is the
last time

I'm not ready
but I've received

enough. If enough
is enough. Have I

given enough?

What I didn't know
is how surprised I'd be

to find her silver hair
on my own blue scarf.

Delighted and afraid
to see it sparkle

like talcum
in an actor's hair.

Shakkei: Borrowed View

In my mother's window
the single

white peak,
everywhere

aspiring, Hood
whittled sharp.

I lay out the bright Tarot

before breakfast. What's that
on your bed? she asks.

Do the cards scare her the way
the flare of matches

can? Shape
shifting, she blocks

the light. My mind
leaps up

to the guardian firs
where the margins

of the Japanese
garden burn clean

with the beauty
of extra white.

Strange Facts

I know grass has a distress
call and crows recognize

human faces, but what do they
feel? I ask them when they

approach, but they're mistrustful
as sudden widows.

Do you think the birds
are talking to us? my sister asks

after an hour of silence
in the car. Unknowable

as the crows. We're driving to
Neskowin on the Oregon coast

the way we do every year.
I'm older, so I always answer.

Yes, I say, but I don't think we
know how to listen.

No Curtains

Alone in the country
where 9-1-1
would never find
the long gravel drive
to my sister's farm

I'm a party of one
collecting blue eggs
and rummaging
in the pantry
for beeswax stubs.

I haven't heard
the ghost yet. I'll
hear her sweep the stairs.
For a centerpiece,
plastic whistles

and a pile
of dinosaur toys,
my nephew's blue nail polish
and Manic Panic dye.
Bach cello sonatas, Yo Yo
Ma secretly sonorous.
A sweet pot of vichyssoise,
that white velvet name.

I switch on the lights
in the cold hallway
lie down in the big white
bed to sleep
with all the lights on
and a junior
baseball bat at my hip.

More afraid
of the living
than of the dead.
The house a bright
ocean liner in the black
Oregon night,
naked hayfields
threshed only today.

Over the mirror
Rumi warns:
People are passing between
the worlds. Don't
go back to sleep!

Not Yet Across

Why do we choose utterance
if the whole world is in flames.

So prepared for chance
but not yet across

I open the window
thinking of a friend's question

When are you going to live?
Our discourses compete, swirl

in a figure 8 stirred into a misty mirror.
Can chaos and calm co-exist?

Don't drop the ladle it says
in the hexagram for Shock.
*

In photographs of water
are still waves an oxymoron?

The light tonight is butter yellow
a winter color, the best it can offer

a pulse or two
of steady, lukewarm brightness.

A dim stove light.
Then hot embers tossed

in the air like fire balloons
rising over the ocean.

Courting

Songbirds are hiding in the holly bush
trying to get it right. Hitting the same notes

over and over. Courting the empty air.
What are the odds for birds?

Surely females make those calls,
how often do they fail?

Detail

"Lemons, Oranges and a Rose" (1633), Francisco Zurbarán

Bone-black steeping
a basket of oranges,

I saw only
the background.

Tamped down.
Restrained.

I was not awake
until then.

Becoming a refugee.
Aware of the deep

moan of timbers
and the sea's brewed threat.

Eight-Minute Essay

In an era of peak performance, I should be able to use eight minutes productively. Generate a lyric response to the sun and the green pond throbbing over its brim on the windblown drive to the station, head half out the window like a dog. Joy mixed with climate change every time I turn on the tap. Everything tainted by thoughts of long- and short-term. The usual obsessions paling. Looking for an answer in the intricate puzzle faces of blue and yellow pansies as I stand in line for the bus. Thinking of refugees in the deserts and oceans. Not taking anything for granted. Trying to stay inside the three times (past, present, and future) at all times.

— Two —

Northwest Passage

I'll never come back
for good.
I know that now.

Between us, East coast
and West, the jagged American
ranges, sugared nibs sharp

over the loose curls
of the Missouri, then the curtain
of rain, that medial, tinsel door.

I try to read your shape behind it
the way I read books
longing for an explanation.

Push-Pull Summer

In the silence, small planes
purr along the coast

dragging banners of DARLING
over Shelter Island.

Clear decisions, Clare says, squinting
at a landscape of tiny red figures.

She bows over her laptop with a stack
of index cards full of sloppy Japanese.

Where's the heat? Jamaal asks. He knows
the answer. In the repetition, he mutters.

His cherry-haired boyfriend sleeps with his ear
against a long cafe table, remembering a kiss.

His wet glass making the second figure 8 I've seen
today. Another infinity. The first a blue

rubber band twisted at Sunset Beach
where my sister pointed out a double rainbow

over the ocean. What's it mean? she asks
the Ethiopian driver standing next

to a long black car. What's it mean?
He shrugs. He could be

ferrying the dead. No,
he says. No secret.

Trans Portrait

Below a bruise in the darkening sky
Orlando is a stag in the fog. Formal
in black tie. Blushing,
making a departure.
Does s/he have proof
of her chastity? Is there any
contraband in her mind?
What did she collect
as a boy? Why can't s/he fly?

Running Brush

On the sails of a late
boat, light

clear and extreme,
bourbon gold

or is it Scotch? In comes
the shook foil of water.

Look it up—
all the details are there

and photographic proof
of how you have lived.

You write down
your own version

of events. Wanting to
take something in.

To dissolve inside
the sound

of a tree in the wind.
You want to see

your body in front of you.
You want to see it float.

Doing Rounds

All these chores like nursing
a fancy drink,

I rake the kindergarten-
red leaves in the Japanese

garden, then listen
to the AAA mechanic—

his son's getting a master's
in Literature at Temple—while

he dabs bluish dust
off the battery.

We study it together
like surgeons.

Across the canyon
the hardwoods thin,

losing their fire,
paring back,

and time divides safely
into Red Sea walls.

Chore after chore
I try not to think,

only to enter
the amplitude,

to see lavender and know
nothing at all.

Mirabilia

The thick sexy mascara inside
the red and yellow tulip cups.

The jokes of the little brown birds
in the underbrush.

That's consciousness!
an ex says, reading a line

about kissing. We should all
live like poets!

No longer telling me
I'm crazy for imagining

what other people think.
Are you writing this down?

she asks. You have all the data
you need. People love this stuff!

As if everything were ethnographic
data. Amazed, seeing

nothing but *mirabilia*.
Unexpected celebrations!

She's right. Even poets
should live like poets, but we

get sad. Wish for more.
Chuck oil on the fire.

Passenger Pigeon #3

If loss had a sound, it might be

the sweeping feathers of the great

flocks, two billion at times,

cash being shuffled, greenbacks,

whatever a billion is,

that childish slang for infinity.

Nearly silent, a premonition.

I don't know how much more

we need to learn about loss.

Holding it lightly,

the fast beating

heart about to stop.

Dark clouds blocking the light

over Boston an hour at a time.

Pink Night

Does what happens
in dreams

stay in dreams?
An empty violin case

on the water
is open. Unhinged.

What is it about?
It is not about.

You walked away
but it wasn't you.

Ready about, you said.

You were in your
house, but it wasn't

your house. You were
walking into the water.

I wanted to
dress you,

but I couldn't find
the right clothes.

Did we love you not
for what you did

but for what you were?
What were you?

Tunnel

Another phone call that I
cannot answer. I can hear

her voice, but she can't
hear mine. She says my name

wavery as a ghost, a little afraid,
too brave to say so.

I want to fly out
but I force myself not to.

She wants my company. Trusts me.
As ever, impatient, she will not wait

for an attendant. Undeterred
in the dark, she clutches

the phone like a prisoner.
Carving her way out.

Great Island Common, New Castle, NH

The sky Irish gray, the water refuses
to lie still, rustles, turns away

among the rocks, shellacked
and black in the shadows.

A black box
of a car, all sealed

up with blackened windows,
slicks past with bagpipes trailing

half grief, half joy, almost
lifting me off the ground.

Small Gold Figure

Arms spread wide
running across the spine

of a red book—Artemis
in a shower of arrows?

Ten years old
my principal desire

to be good
in a noble, boyish way.

Now I cannot think
of anything significant

to say, everyone
like someone

I've met before; only
the homeless look interesting.

How to read—
left to right or right to left?

Sunwise or moonwise?

Self-Portrait

With no arms.

A lace wall.

With words.

With closed

mouth. With eyes

and no mouth.

As a book.

With words

from head

to foot.

With closed

mouth pursed

to say.

Lips sealed

in wax.

As a book

open as a mouth.

Teeth like heels

in an empty hall.

Aporia

At dusk, a car
with no lights

flashes me to
put mine on.

What are you certain
of when you are

certain of nothing? How to turn
the wheel of fortune?

The original has to destroy
itself before the replica

can appear far
from that location.

What's my superposition?

We've mapped only
a fraction of the universe.

The rest we call dark.
Everyone in my dreams

is self-assured.
Words rising from

their mouths, open
as if they are singing.

I Make Out

with a beautiful woman
on the beach.

Am I a guy this time?
She keeps coming back

to kiss me again
though she has to leave.

Across the channel, people
in rock caves are watching.

It is the end of the world.
My mother is sleeping in a crib.

Erasing *Moby Dick*

                     I thought I would sail
     the watery part of the world

                    Whenever I
find myself   grim   whenever it is a damp

drizzly November   whenever I find myself
                   bringing up the rear

deliberately stepping into the street
          I account it   time to
take to the ship

— Three —

Nothing Up My Sleeve

"If you can see them,
they can see you." *One wave*

after another. No room. And so on.
It may not look like that

but it's true. (I think that's what
she said.) Walking down the road

with a mirror, I darken. Turn it
to precede me, about-face, cast sweet

buttercup light on the exposed
neck of the tar curve. Bringing up

the rear, I sweep. Buck up.
Meet myself coming

and going. If you can see
them, they can see

you. It's true. I
hide. Deepen

the magic, keeping it
sleight.

Mine Own

Overtaking us from behind,
a red-tailed hawk, my lucky

sign, swoops to attack.
With one hand, I snatch

it by the neck and drop it
off the bridge to fly.

Mother, heavy now,
a pyramid in a wheelchair

watches a blues
festival at the railing.

The world is a bridge,
build no house upon it,

isn't that what
the Persians say,

I offer when she says
she has no home.

"Is that what they say?"
She never complains.

Look to the lilies of the field,
she said when we were young,

a Catholic koan.
Below my window

as if deep in water
yellow flowers pop up and out

of the black air. Mindful of death,
the wise should not be inclined

to be devoted to mine.
A truck backs and backs again

at mantra speed. She's found
on her knees on the bathroom

floor, speech unclear,
spirits good.

Extra White

Pressing hard, line after
line, gutter by

gutter, Agnes
Martin is raking long

rows of sand into
cloudy cursive,

loosening the beauty
of empty space, *yohaku no bi.*

Waves of ambiguous white wrested
and roiling in the selvedge.

Burn

The night before you died
you said Burn.

I saw a hawk capture
a small bird in its claws.

I joined you in the Hail Mary
and you looked surprised.

Ward off, the Tai Chi move,
you were warding off.

Burn, what's going to burn?
Palms raised

like someone walking
in the dark.

The moment before his death, Takuan
painted the character for dream.

A gold-faced goddess
is polishing her breasts.

I did not cry
but I could not keep

my balance on the grass
of your grave.

Ghost Party

I walk into the stir
of a cocktail party and see myself

across the crowded room
smiling and talking.

Then you, in another small circle,
wearing a beaded white dress

(you're a ghost, so it follows).
Fiercely beautiful

no one else as striking. You wave
and call my name, hinging it,

drawing it out in a sing-song chant.
Trying to wake me up?

Warning me? Making my way
across the room

I'm so glad to see you again
and so surprised to see myself as well.

Future Perfect

Following the birds
to the vanishing point, empty

sky. Nothing happens
but everything happens

inside it. Scrying
where there is nothing

to see. Look! the Nepali
clerk says,

Your change! It's $9.11!
Space moves around

like furniture. Three
dots, three girly bubbles,

and erases them. A gap.
Mind the gap.

Tagred, the Saudi student
who wears a kind of helmet veil

like Athena,
asks me about an action

that will have occurred before
another action in the future.

The Meeting

Do you dream of me
the way I dream of you?

You wait like a friend
in need. In your old polo

coat, the one with the taffy
buttons, hands deep

in the big satin pockets.
Worried, in your thirties,

horn-rims, so serious.
I'm usually in a meeting. I call

you back and you turn
in the street to return.

Calling you back
from the dead.

I'm your friend now
and I catch your arm.

No Beginning

Begin with yes.
A red yes.

Is there volume in a word?
Circumference? Weight?

It has a Norwegian
sound I fear

especially when escorted
by exclamation.

Hesitant, I paste
the sticker—Yes!—

white letters against red—
on my phone,

practice being someone
enthusiastic: Yes?

On the kitchen table, a bouquet
of white irises

wilts into tatters.
Do you want

to save changes?
Yes!

For Love

If you are the querent
you must learn to trust

a woman
in a doorway

too far away to see
without punctuation
*

I'm trying to explain
the situation—my English

is excellent—if you see
a woman in a black boa

in daylight, you should
kiss her; we are

what everyone
is excited about.

The wave did not rise
up, it was just one long

white frill, you know,
the aftermath.

Spoon

After David Hockney

This shape mirrors
the bowl it is in.

A generative restraint?
This spoon in this bowl

is like every spoon
in every bowl, and the first

such spoon ever. It inhabits
the hollow. Luxuriates

like a loose tongue, shines
haloes and enshrines itself.

Silent Letter

Gold light pulsing
from a cloud, the pond

flicks off and on. Dit dot.
What can't you say?

Thought tearing away
from language

leaving a snakeskin
of interest.

What is the world
without language?

You track the answer,
willing to be wrong.

No Mind

I wake up to the breathing
of the man who walks

behind me in kinhin,
the one with the oxygen

tank who nods
at Bokar Rinpoche's

idea that there is no
mind. No spot

of light. No self.
Labored. Scarce.

I can't swallow
in the silence.

Autonomic goes
conscious

and I can't.
In college,

my nemesis sometimes sat
on the bathroom sink

with a palette of eye
shadow, smiling

in the long silence.

Dark

Let's agree on the science.
Let's look at the cost.

It was dawn.
They put a quilt

on the stretcher.
It was already hard to remember

what she'd been like.

Everything turns away.
The ocean sighs

in its sleep.
Receives the wind.
*

I know about regret.
Is that needed?

She always made
a coconut cake at Easter

in the shape of a lamb
as if she were under a spell.
*

I wrote thank you letters.
Stopped to see the kingfisher

chitter and dive into the salt marsh,
trees the color of dried blood.

You have asked for our help,
the spirits said. I had forgotten.
*

The giant black whale
was disappointingly other.

It rose up slowly. Looked right
at me. I did not feel joy.
*

The surveyor's pink ribbons
fluttering near the pond.

Dead leaves, dear leaves
saying vespers.

We didn't have enough
time, we said.

How much
did we need?

She Loves You

She hadn't finished her dream
so I finished it for her.

I wanted it to be lucid
so that she could move there

as she couldn't otherwise.
I wanted to give it to her

as a gift, so I worked
all night on it.

I made her able to fly.

Green to the Very Door

Sunset like a fire festival
in the pond

she appears by my side

silent the way
ghosts are, wishing

to speak.

What don't you know
that you think you know?

The quick happy chatter of
finches in the underbrush

makes you want to
hold your breath.

If You Were a God

and you were to us,
all the prefixes applied:
omni-, un-, and all-.

All powerful, then gone
as Eckhart said of god:
becoming and unbecome.

Erasing Herself as needed.
Thus, or am I thinking of therefore,

that vulva of dots.
Yesterday, a large hawk

sated in a tree, prey
torn up in the grass.

Diamond Sutra

Provincetown, Massachusetts
So you should think of all the fleeting world:
a star at dawn… / a phantom and a dream.

In the empty parking lot at Herring Cove,
I'm a long spring shadow, gangly

as a Modigliani. The sun dropping fast,
I look for whales the way you look

for a sign. Nothing off the tip
of the cape, probably deep

in a merry *squantum*. There's
a town full of women behind me

looking for love, even if I'm sulky and
star-proof, waiting for my own soul

to come down Commercial, jerky
as a shirt on a line, a regular Communion

wafer, its gay pink innards sizzling
like neon while I sip a Coke at Spiritus.

Notes

"A Step Nearer" alludes to Frank O'Hara's "A Step Away from Them."

"North Sea High Tide" is by Simon Carter, a contemporary British painter.

Japanese sand gardens share in the aesthetic of *yohaku no bi*, "the beauty of extra white" or the "beauty of empty space."

"Running Brush" is the translation of "Zuihitsu," a genre that includes random notes.

"Mirabilia": *plural noun*, Latin: marvels; miracles. (Thanks to Rob Brezsny for the delightful definition of "mirabilia" in his column.)

"One wave after another…." is from Virginia Woolf.

"Mindful of death … to mine" is from the buddhist *Dhammapada*.

Takuan Sōhō (1573–1645) is a well-known figure in the Rinzai school of Zen.

"For Love" is a Robert Creeley title.

"Green to the Very Door" is a line from Wordsworth.

Acknowledgments

Many thanks to Dr. Ross Tangedal, director and publisher, along with editors Brett Hill and Ellie Atkinson, production designer Julia Kaufman, and the entire staff at Cornerstone Press. Special thanks to those who've so generously read my work and shared their knowledge, especially Jen Bervin, Jody Gladding, Rick Jackson, and Mary Ruefle. Particular thanks to Jenny Barber for all her help shaping this manuscript. Thanks also to my poetry friend, Betty Buchsbaum. Special thanks to Greg Lawless. Many thanks to David Rivard for reminding me we don't really know what poetry is. And innumerable thanks to Rick Fox! As always, inexpressible thanks to my family, friends, and teachers of all kinds for your love and support.

Grateful acknowledgment to the editors of the publications where some of these poems first appeared (sometimes in different form). Thanks also to Kristy Bowen of dancing girl press where some of these poems first appeared in a chapbook, *Mirabilia* (2022).

"Burn," *New Letters*, Vol. 78, No. 2, Spring 2012.

"Diamond Sutra," *Cape Cod Poetry Review*, Vol. III, Spring 2016.

"Extra White" and "Great Island Common, Newcastle, NH," "Small Gold Figure," and "Spoon," *Hamilton Stone Review*, Issue No. 35, Fall 2016.

"For Love" and "Future Perfect," *Kenyon Review*, Fall 2013, Vol. XXXV, No. 4.

"Golden Record," *Pittsburgh Poetry Review*, August 2020.

"In Theory," *The Adroit Journal*, Issue #21, January 2020.

"The Meeting," *Apple Valley Review*, Fall 2016.

"No Mind" and "Self Portrait," *Cincinnati Review*, Summer 2013, Vol. 10, No. 1.

"Northwest Passage," *Mudfish*, Issue #13, 2001.

"Not Yet Across," *Mudfish*, Issue #21, 2020.

"Nothing Up My Sleeve" and "Shakkei: Borrowed View," *Stand*, Vol. 12, No. 4, 2014.

"Push-Pull Summer" and "She Loves You," *CutBankOnline*, July 2015.

"TransPortrait," *'Nasty Women' Poets: An Anthology* (Lost Horse Press, 2017).

GAIL HANLON is the author of the chapbooks *SIFT* (2010) and *Mirabilia* (2022). Her poetry has appeared in *The Kenyon Review*, *Ploughshares*, *Cincinnati Review*, *Cut-BankOnline*, *The Iowa Review*, *New Letters*, *Verse Daily*, and *Best American Poetry*, among other journals and anthologies. She won the National Writer's Union Poetry Prize, and has been shortlisted for the Iowa Review Award and *CutBank*'s Patricia Goedicke Prize, and long-listed for *CutBank*'s Chapbook Award, the Tomaž Šalamun Prize at *VERSE*, and OSU's *The Journal* Wheeler Prize, among others.

www.ingramcontent.com/pod-product-compliance
Lightning Source LLC
Chambersburg PA
CBHW031248120626
46545CB00007B/2714